THIS ANIMAL STRING ART PATTERNS BOOK BELONGS TO

....

....

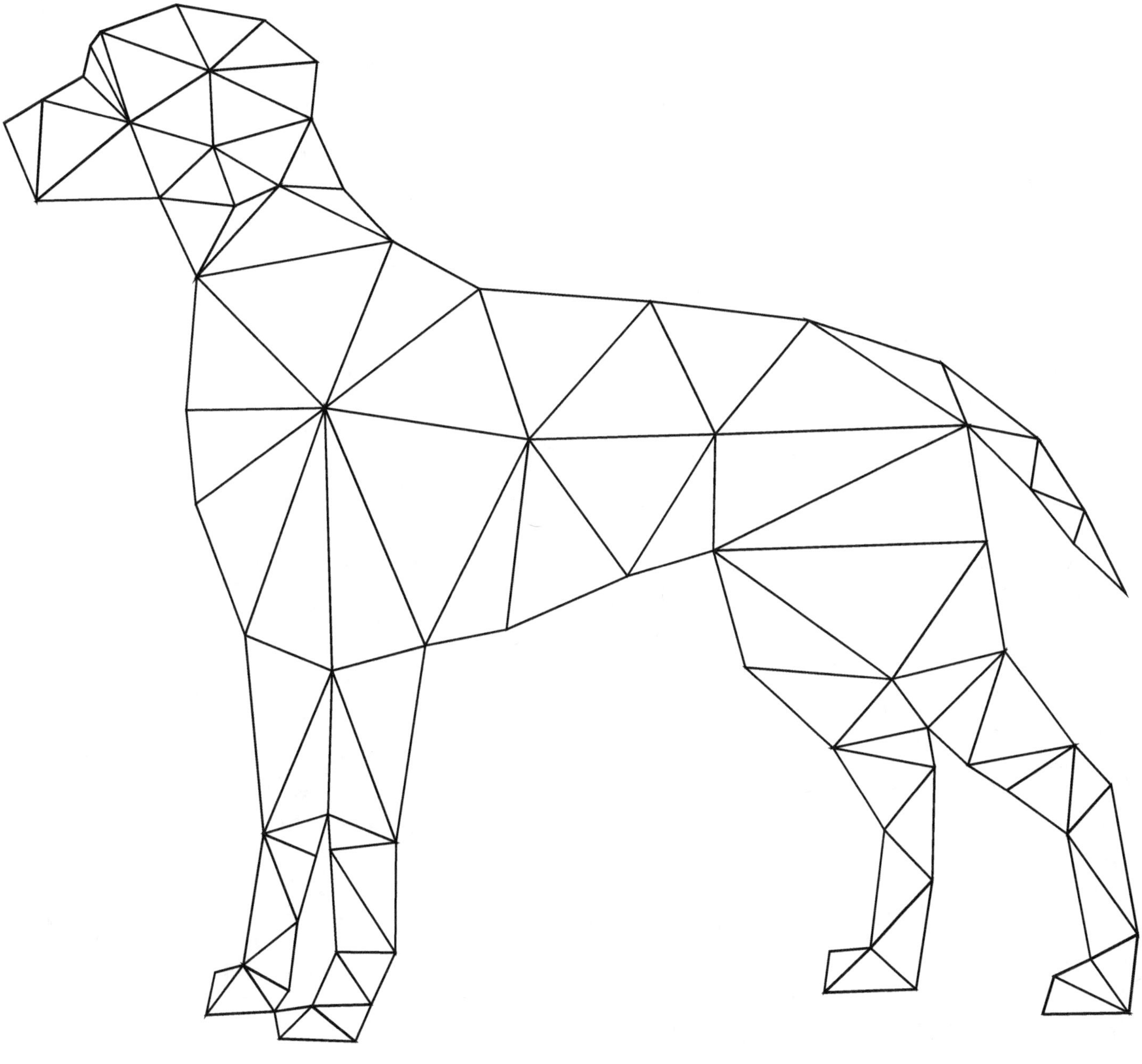

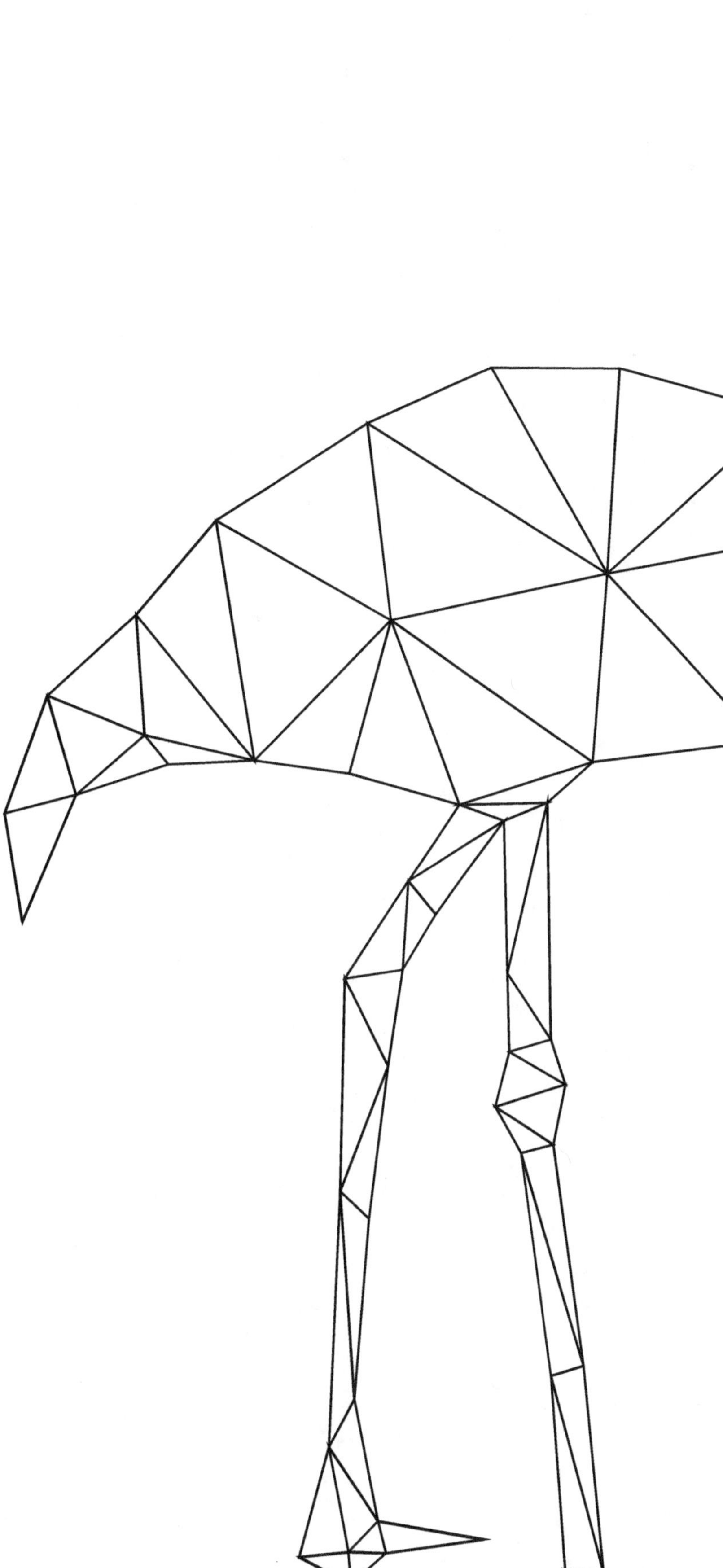

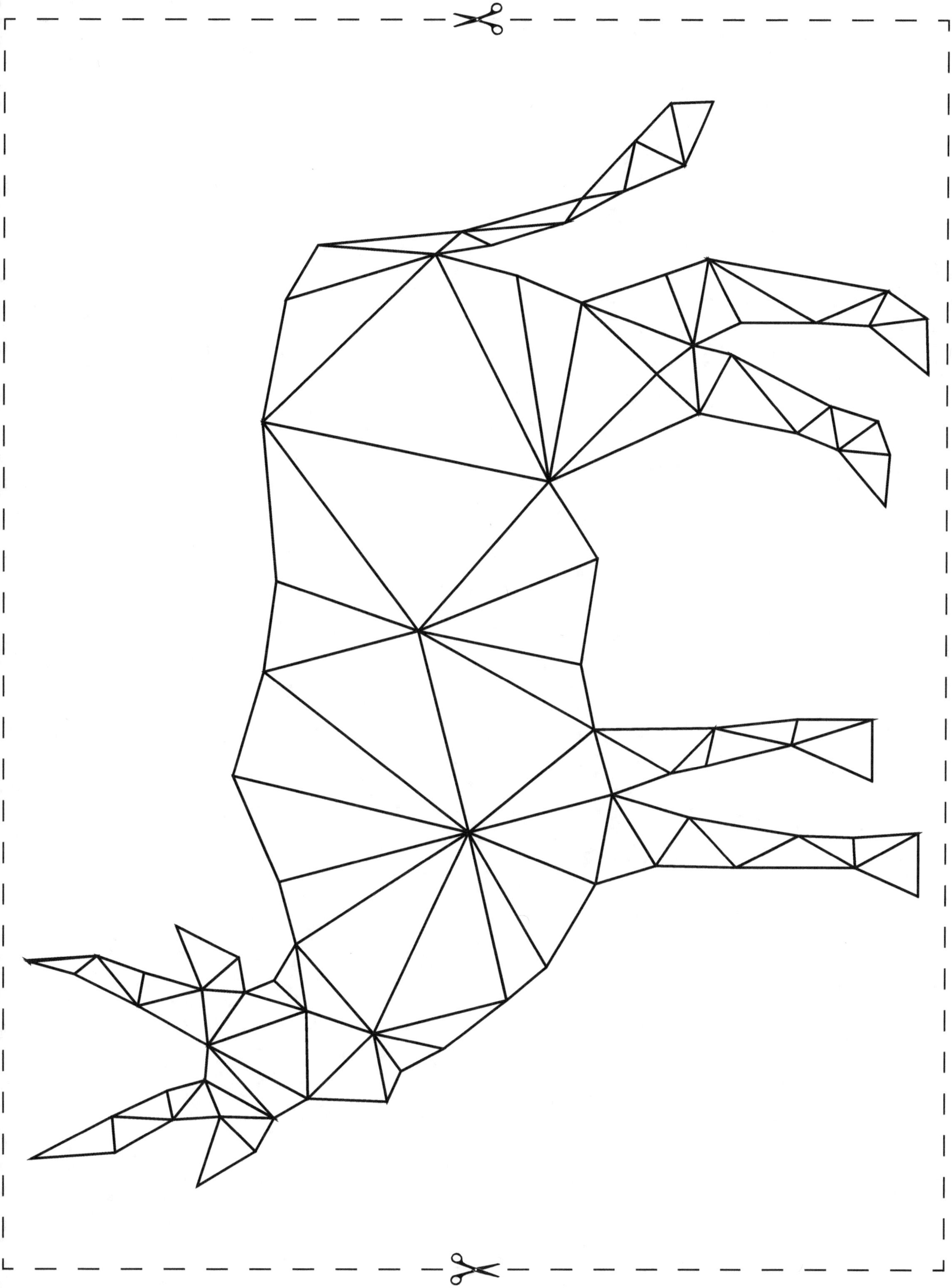

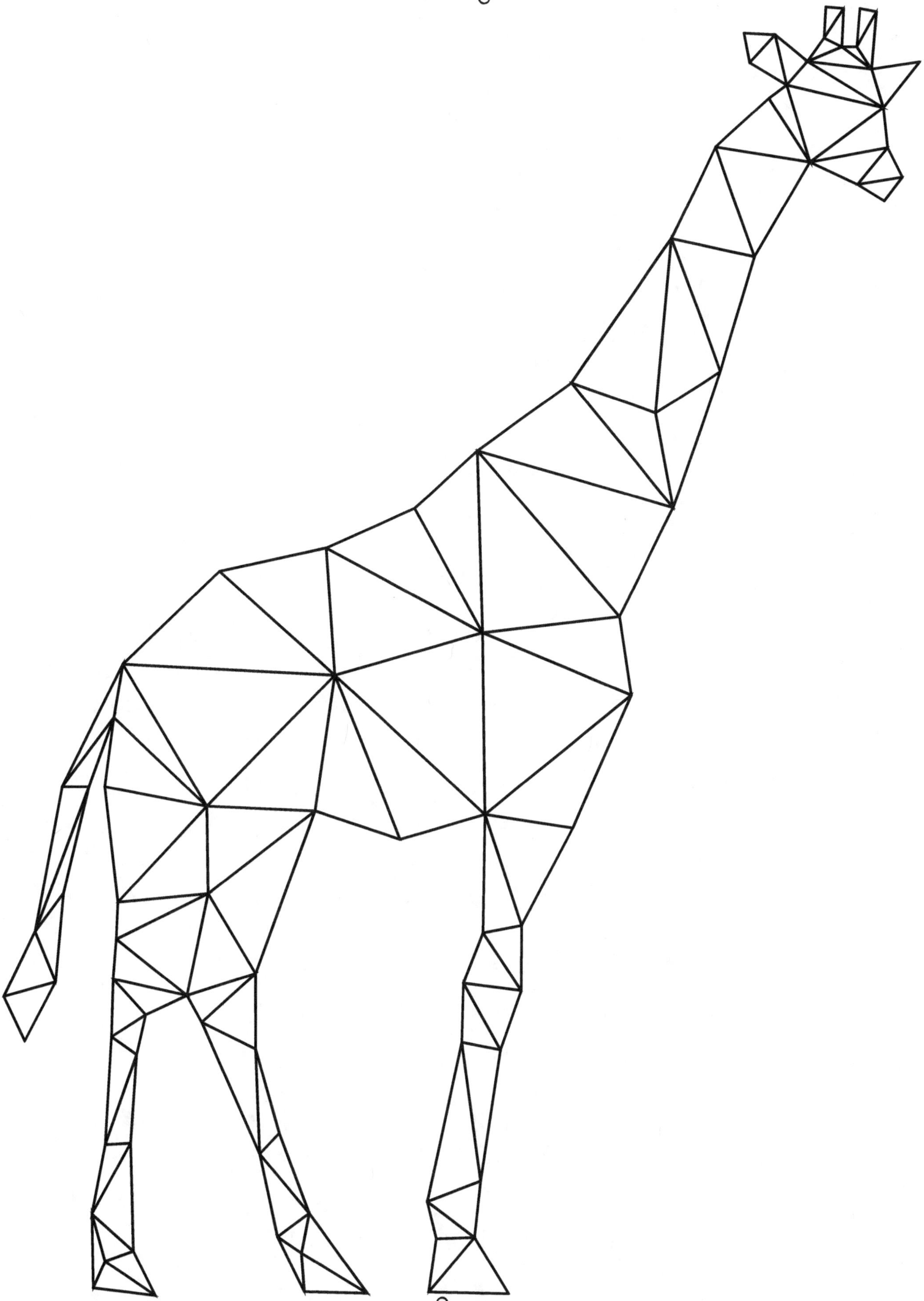

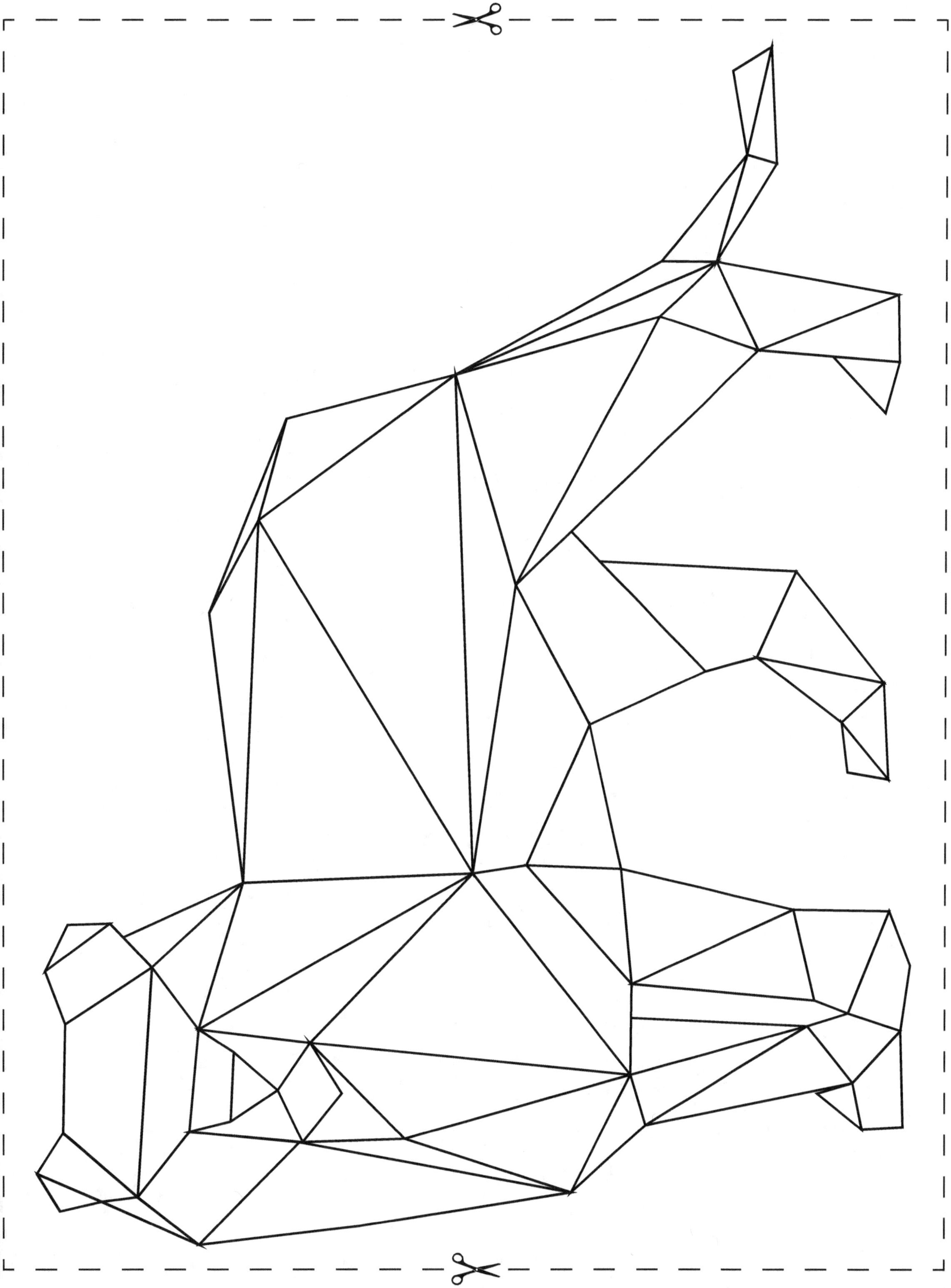

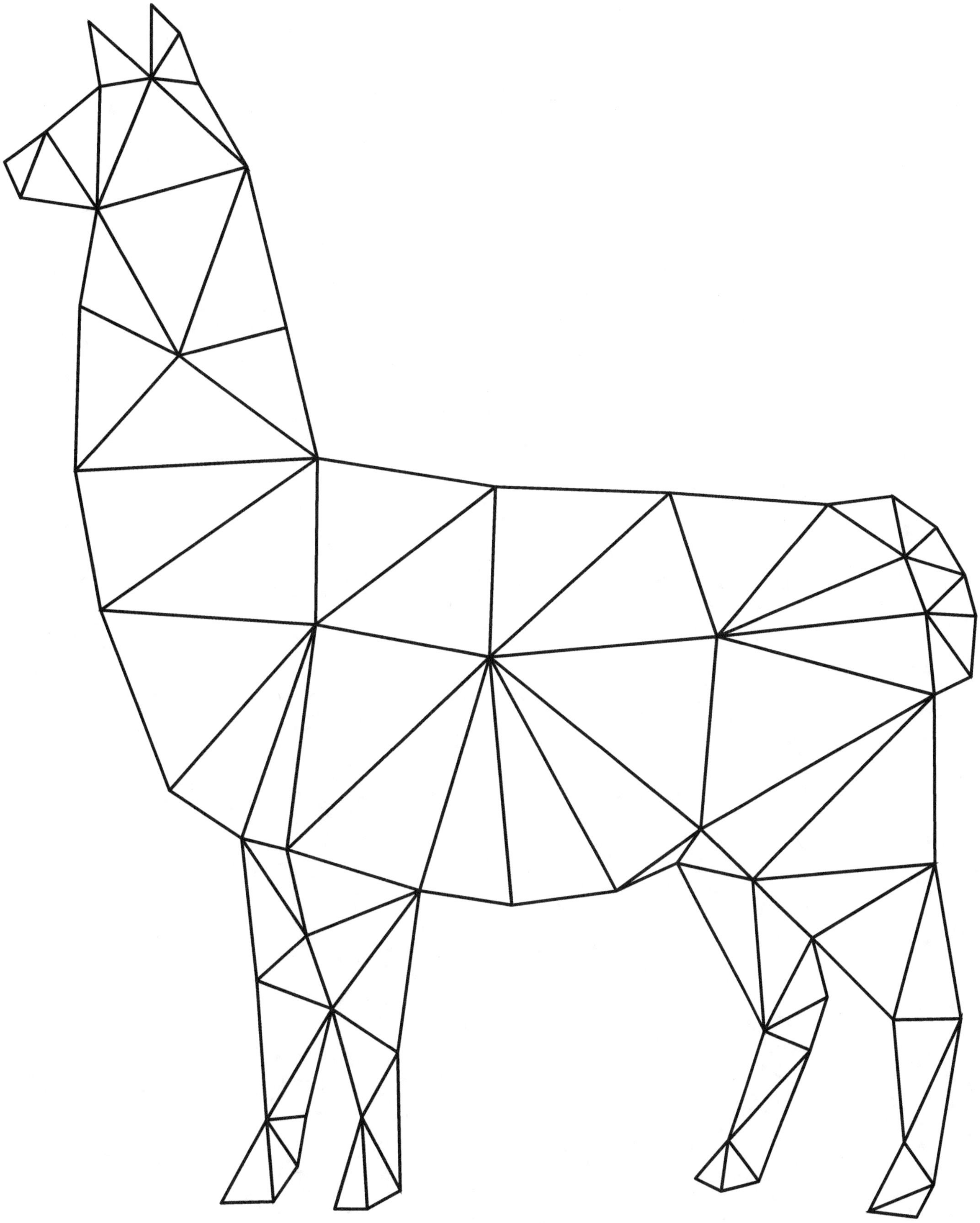

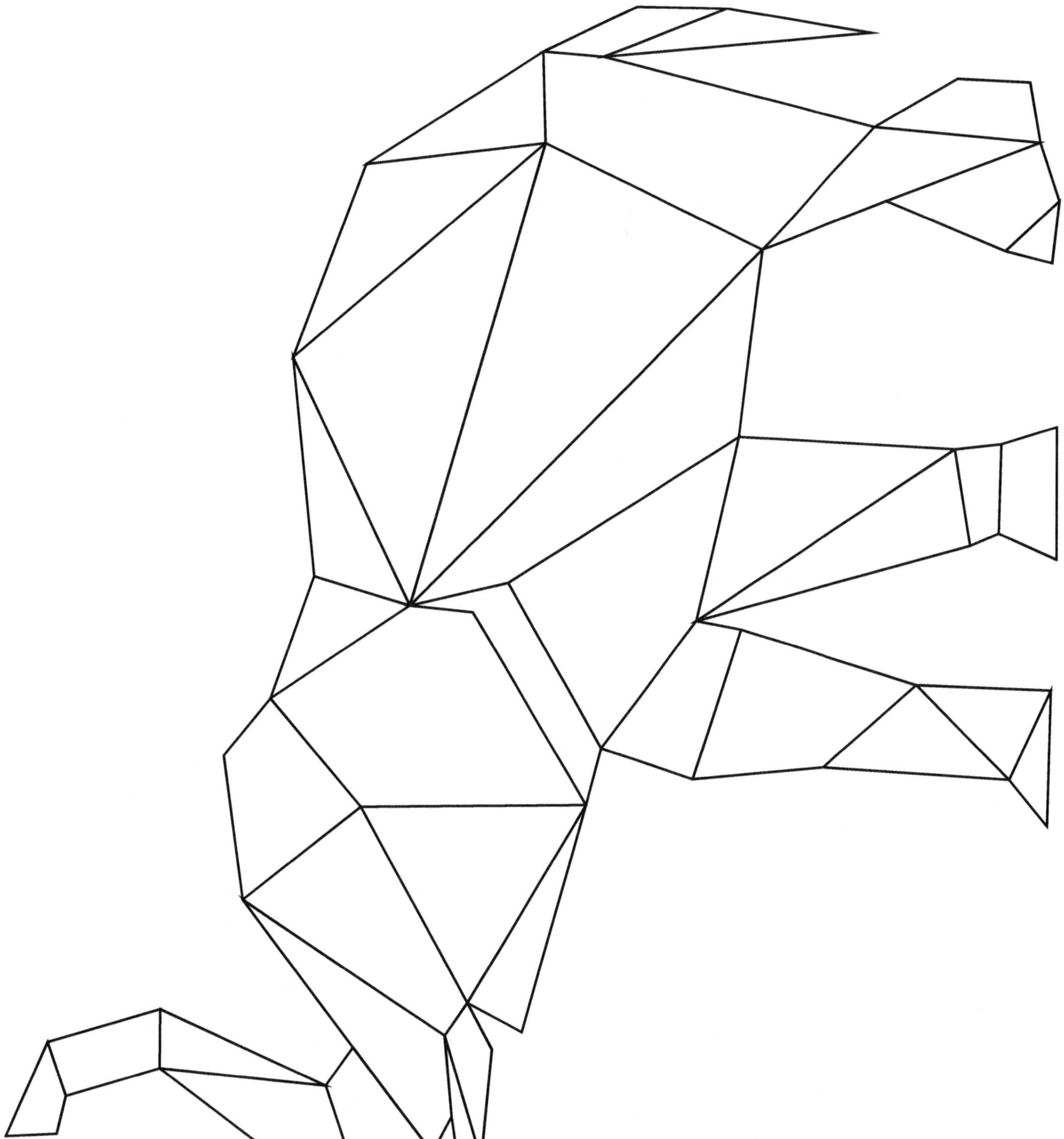

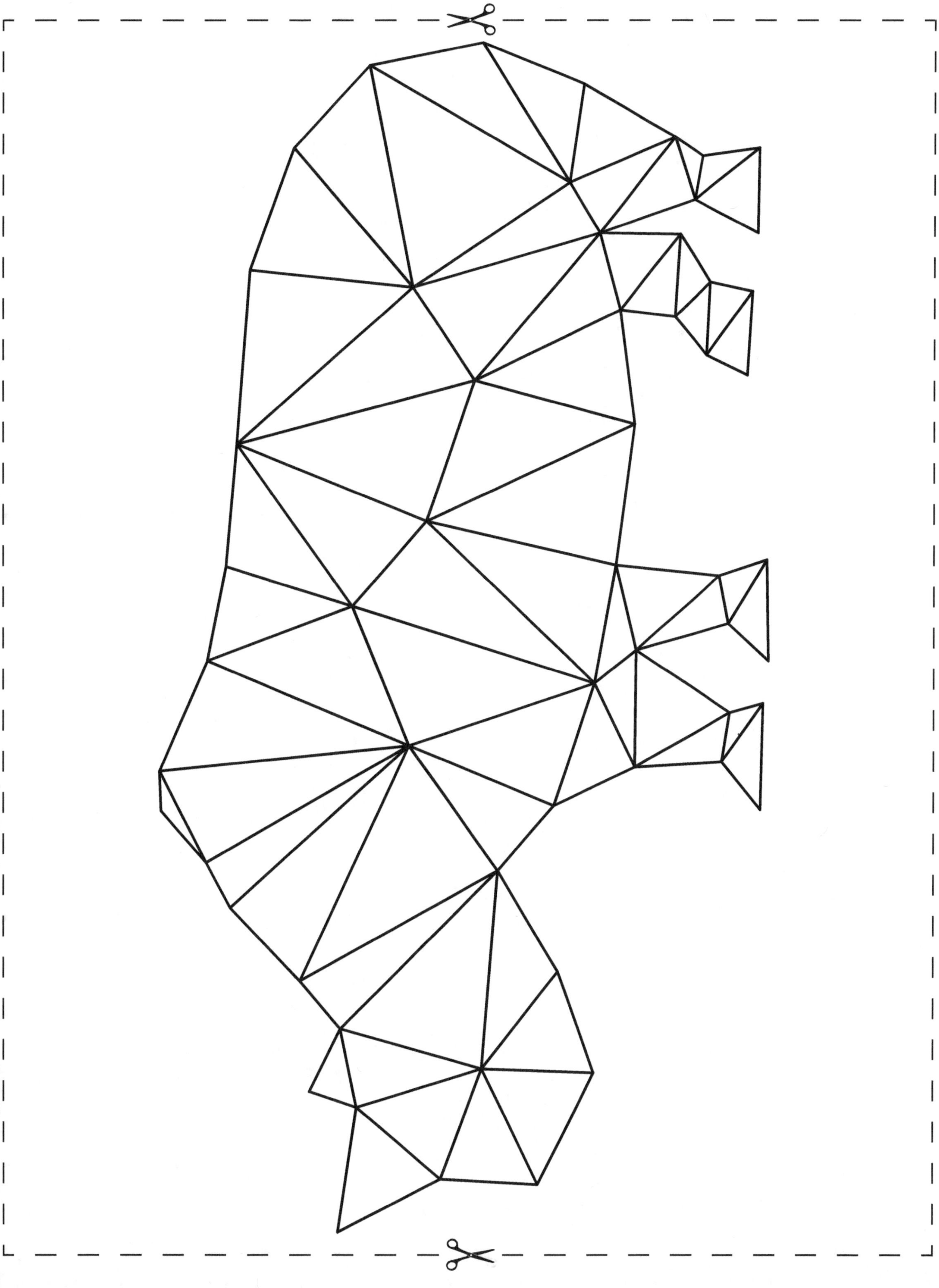

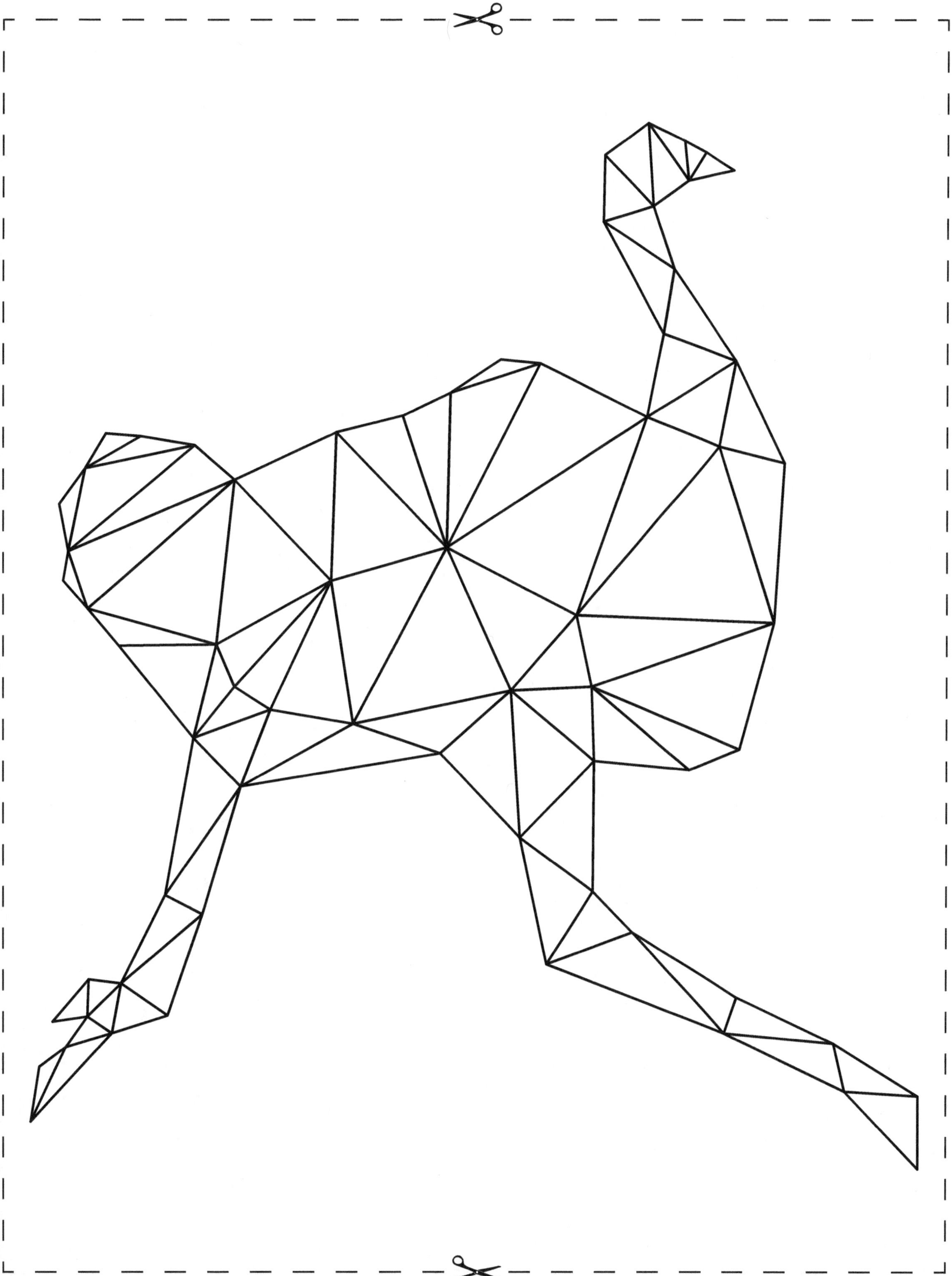

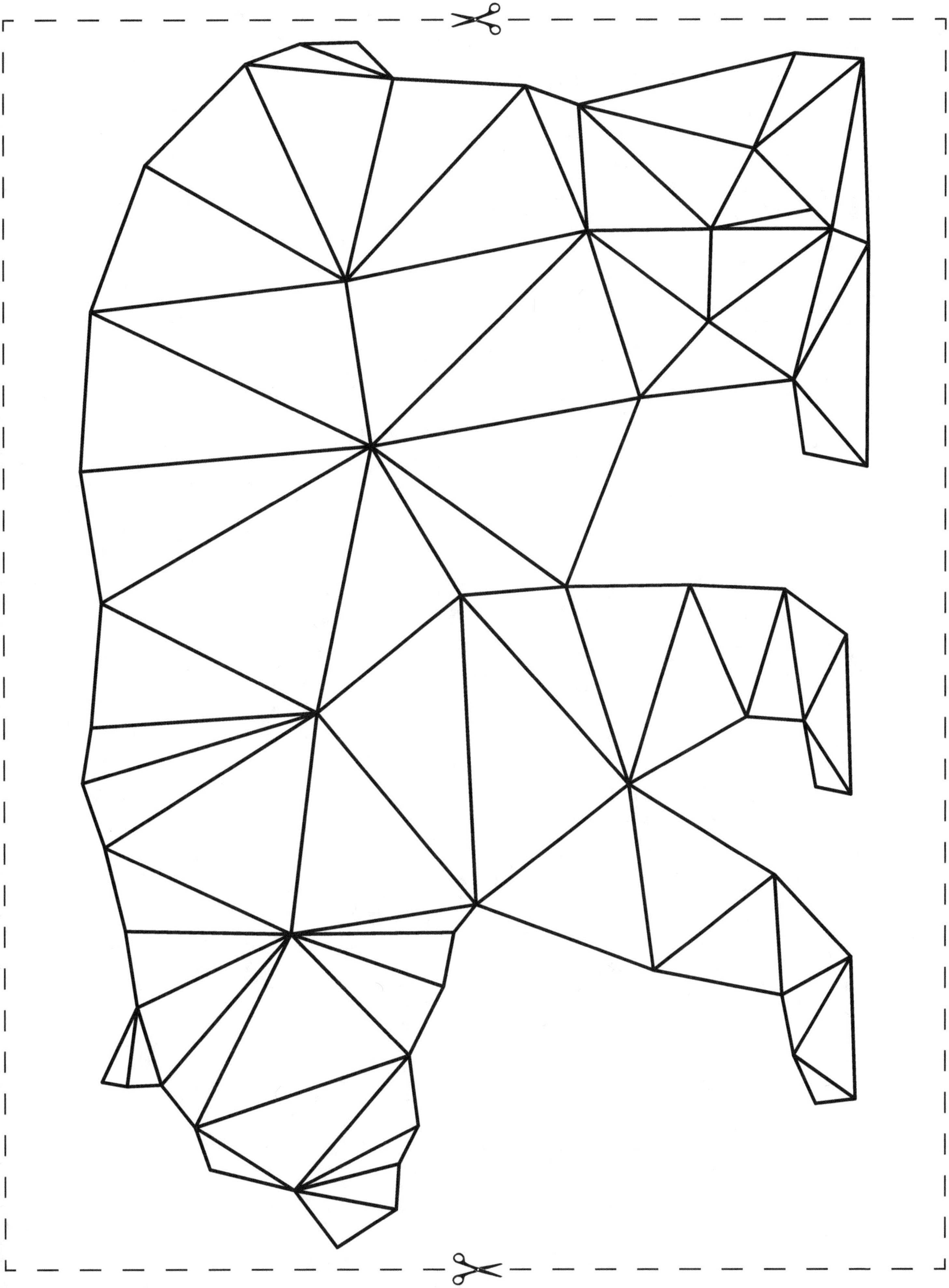

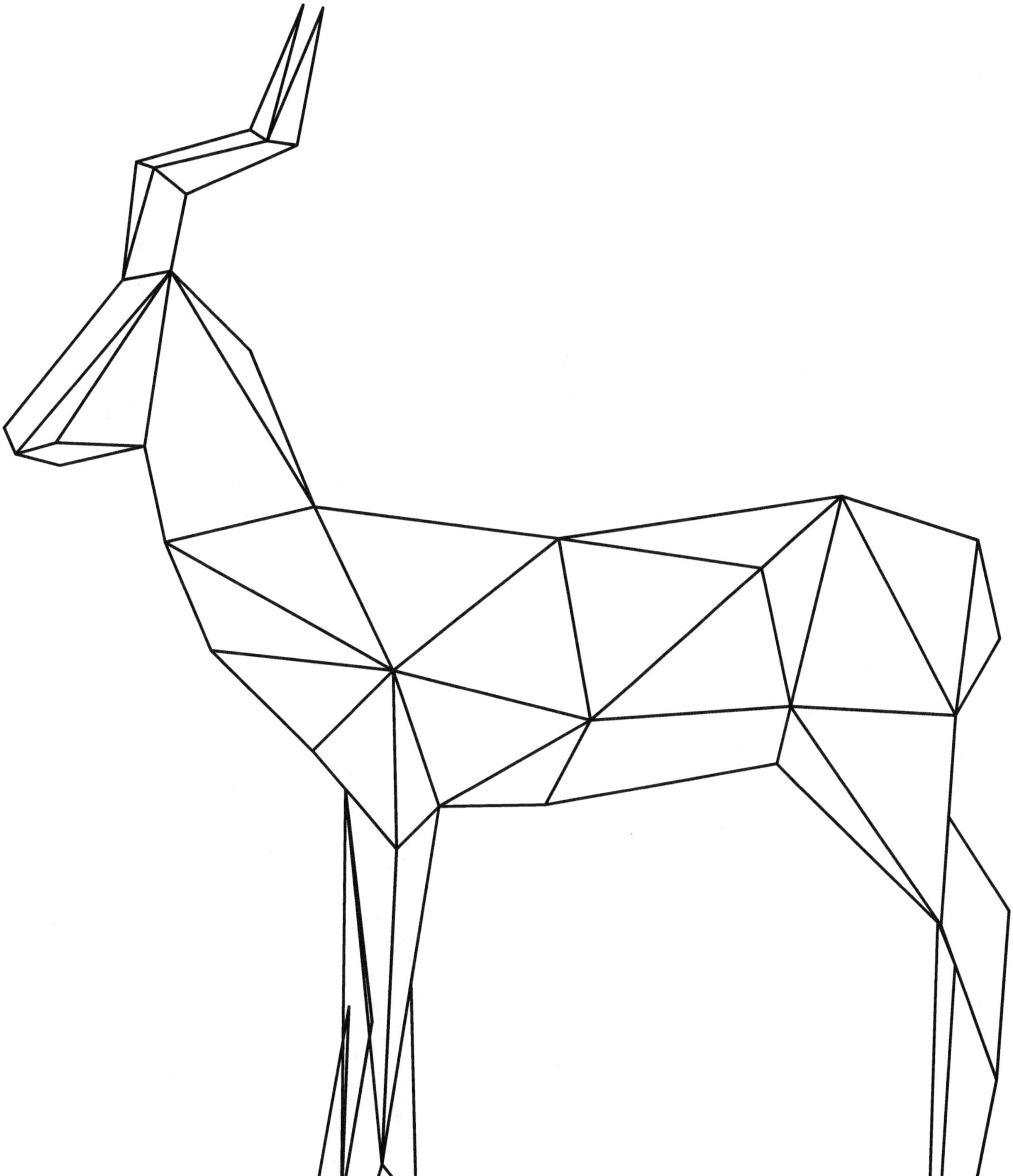

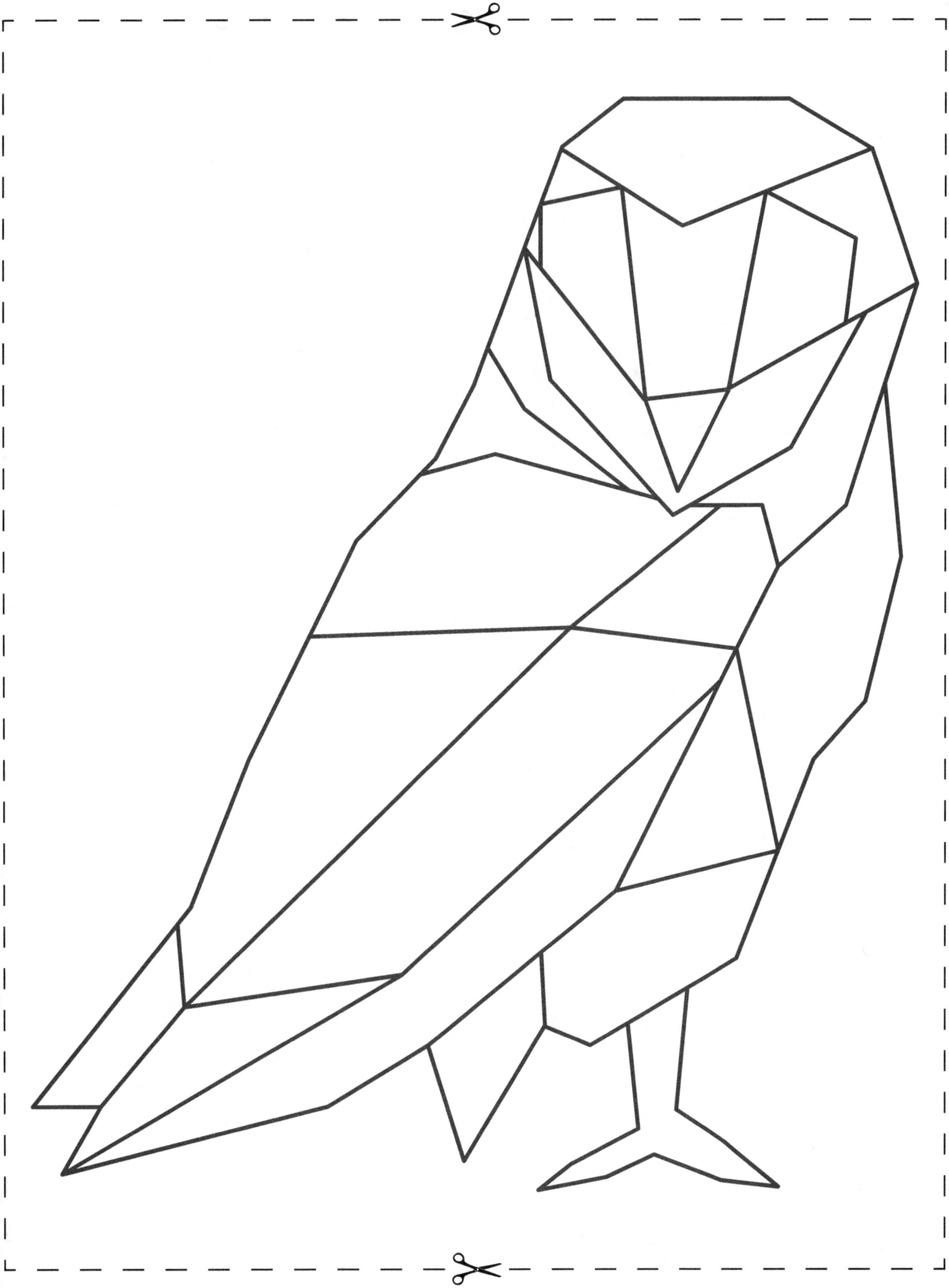

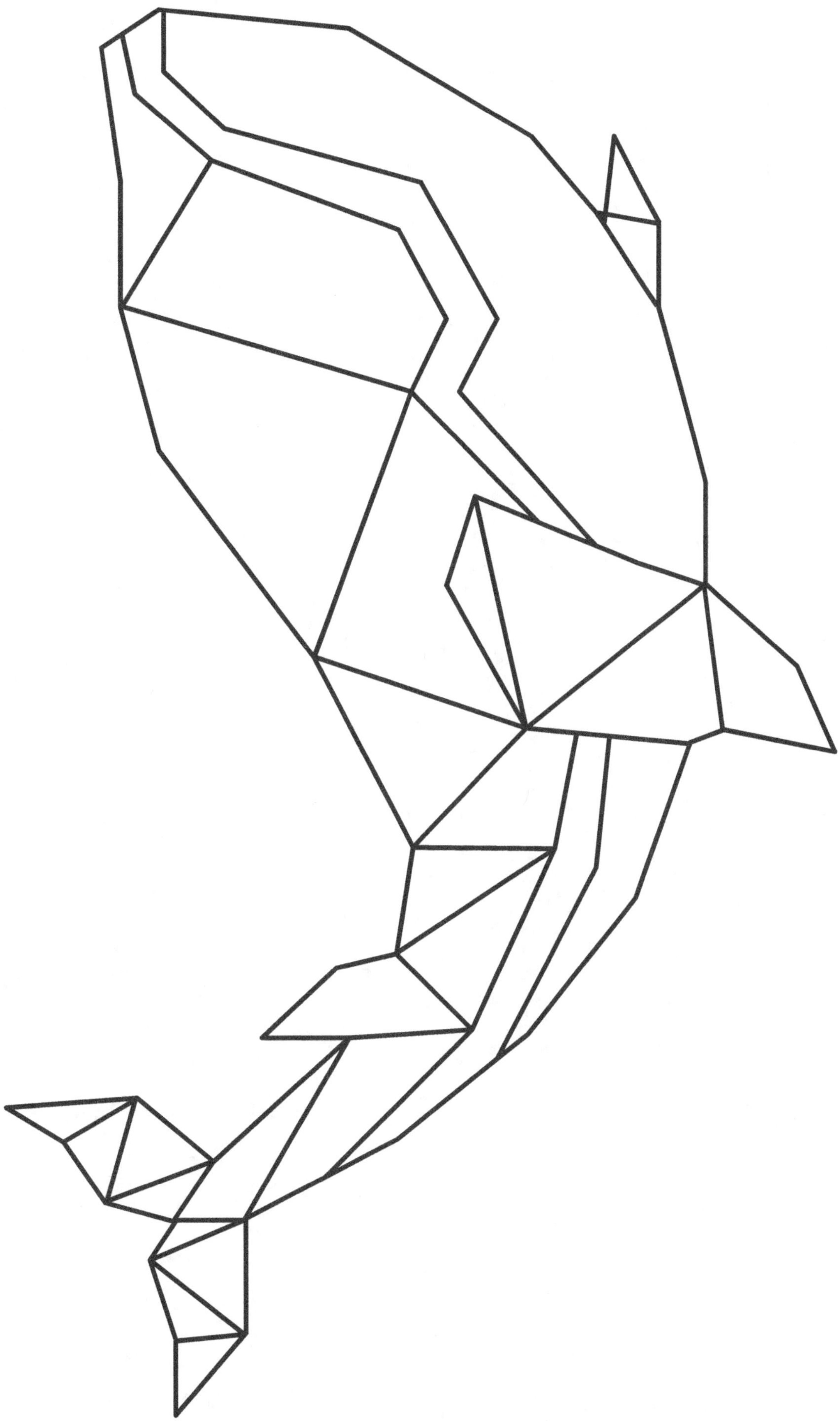

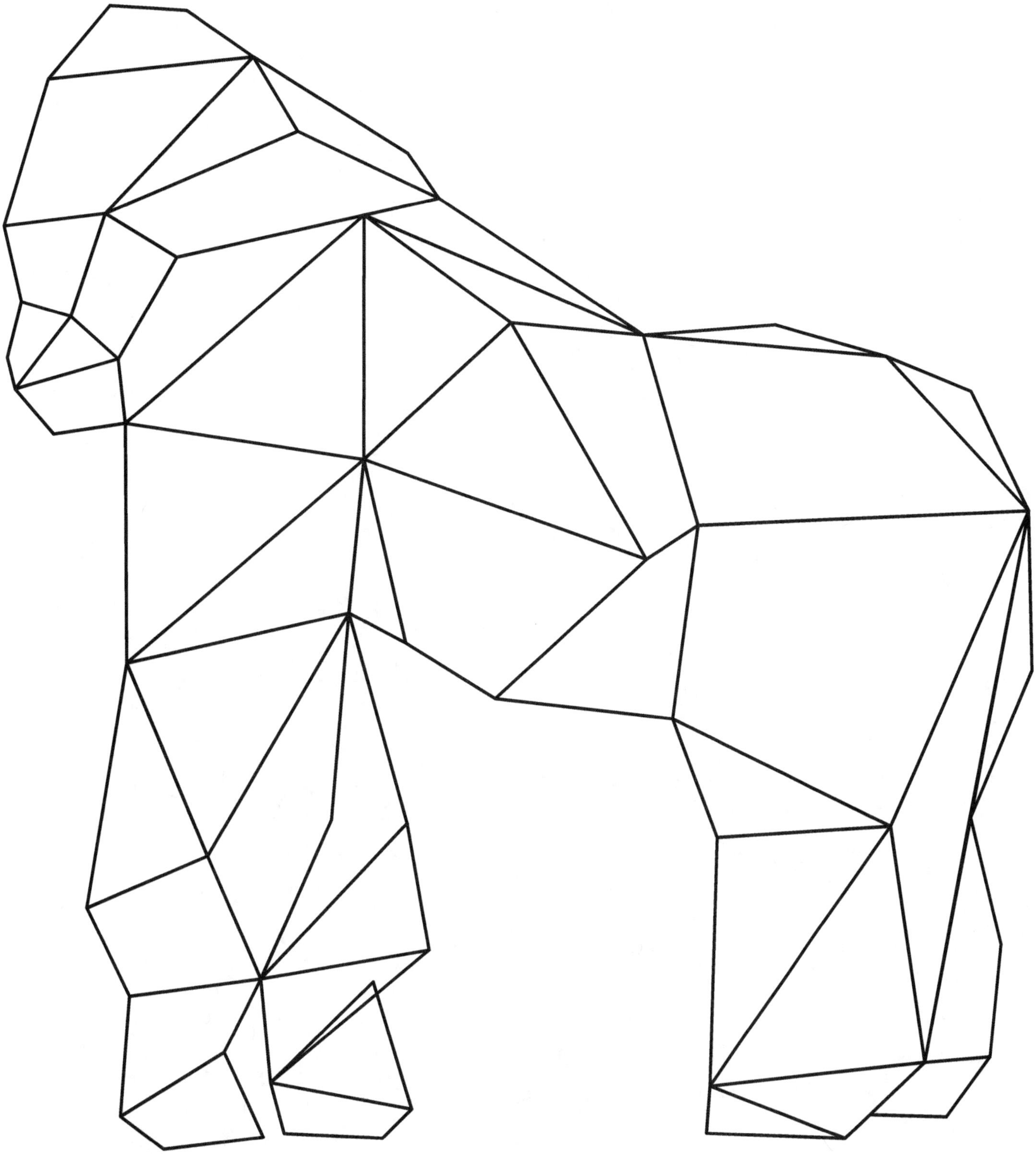

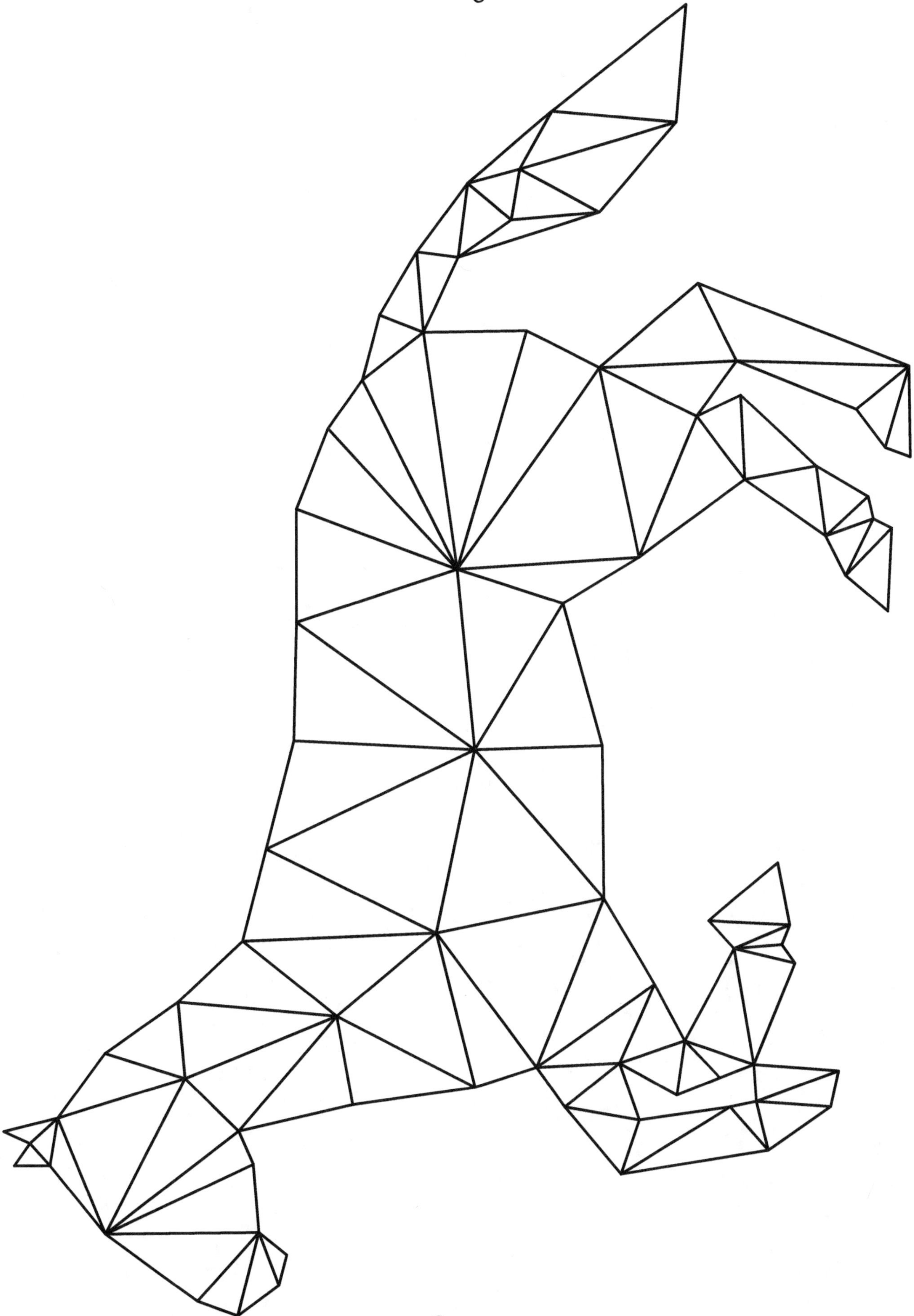

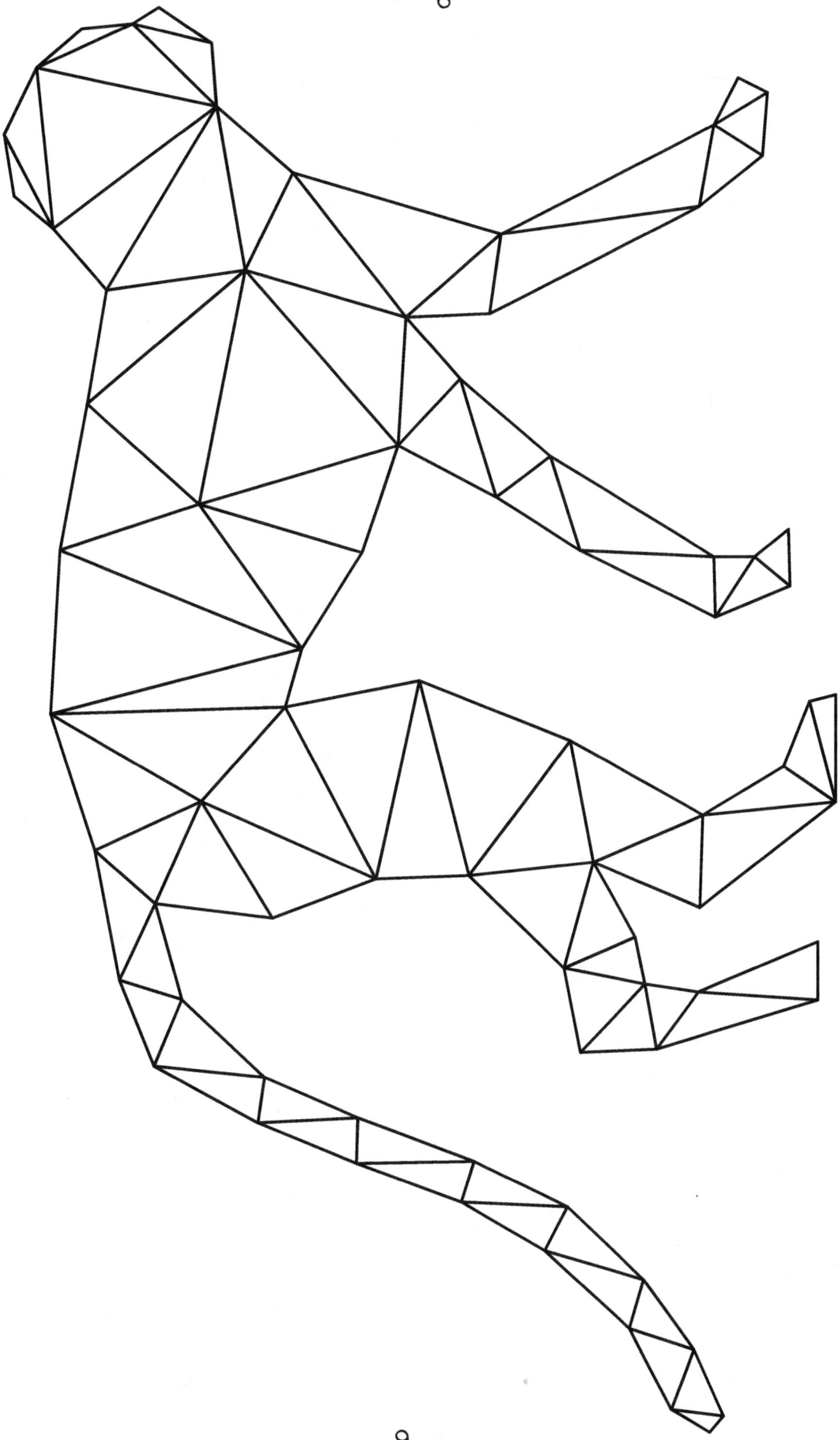

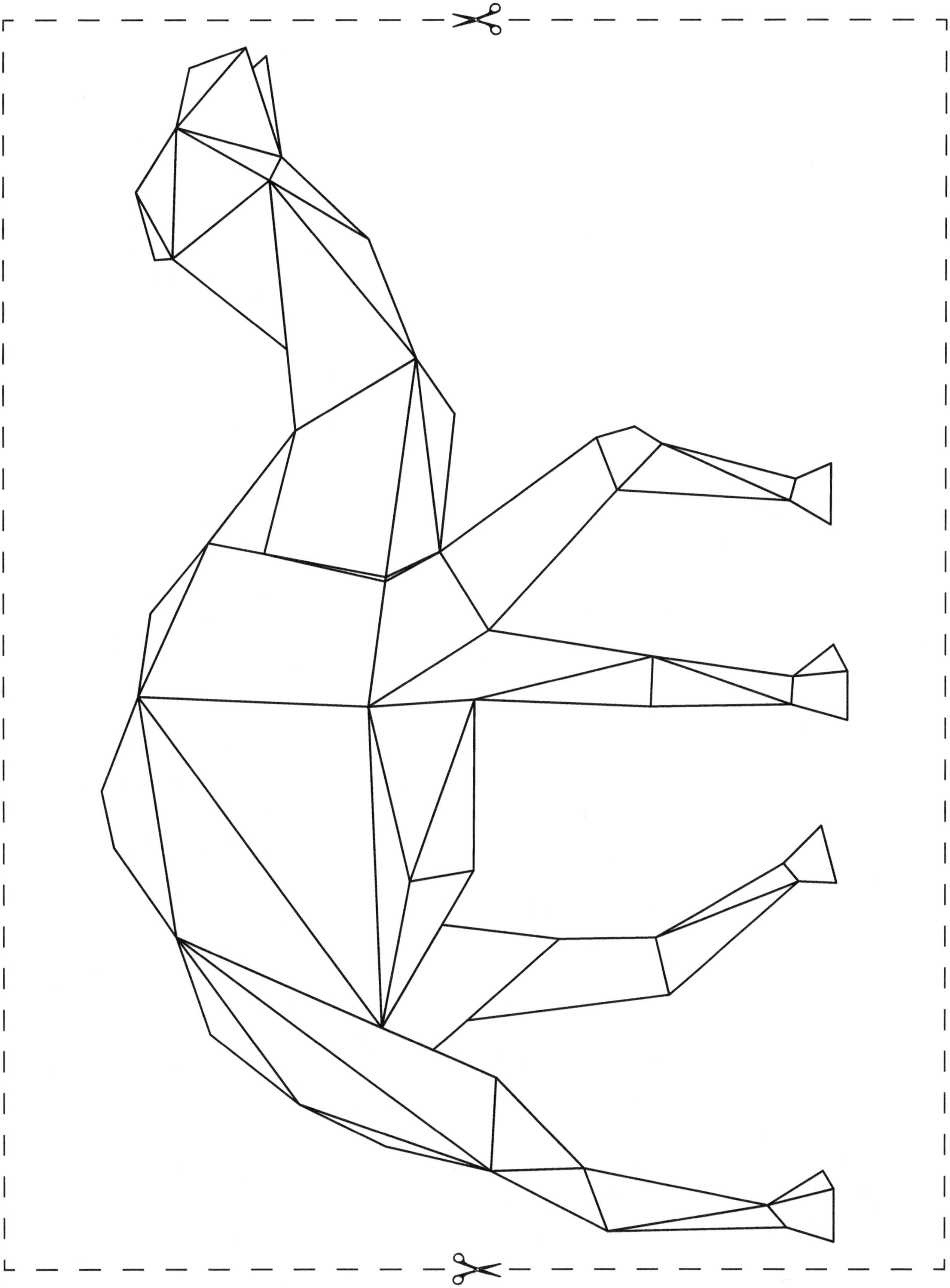

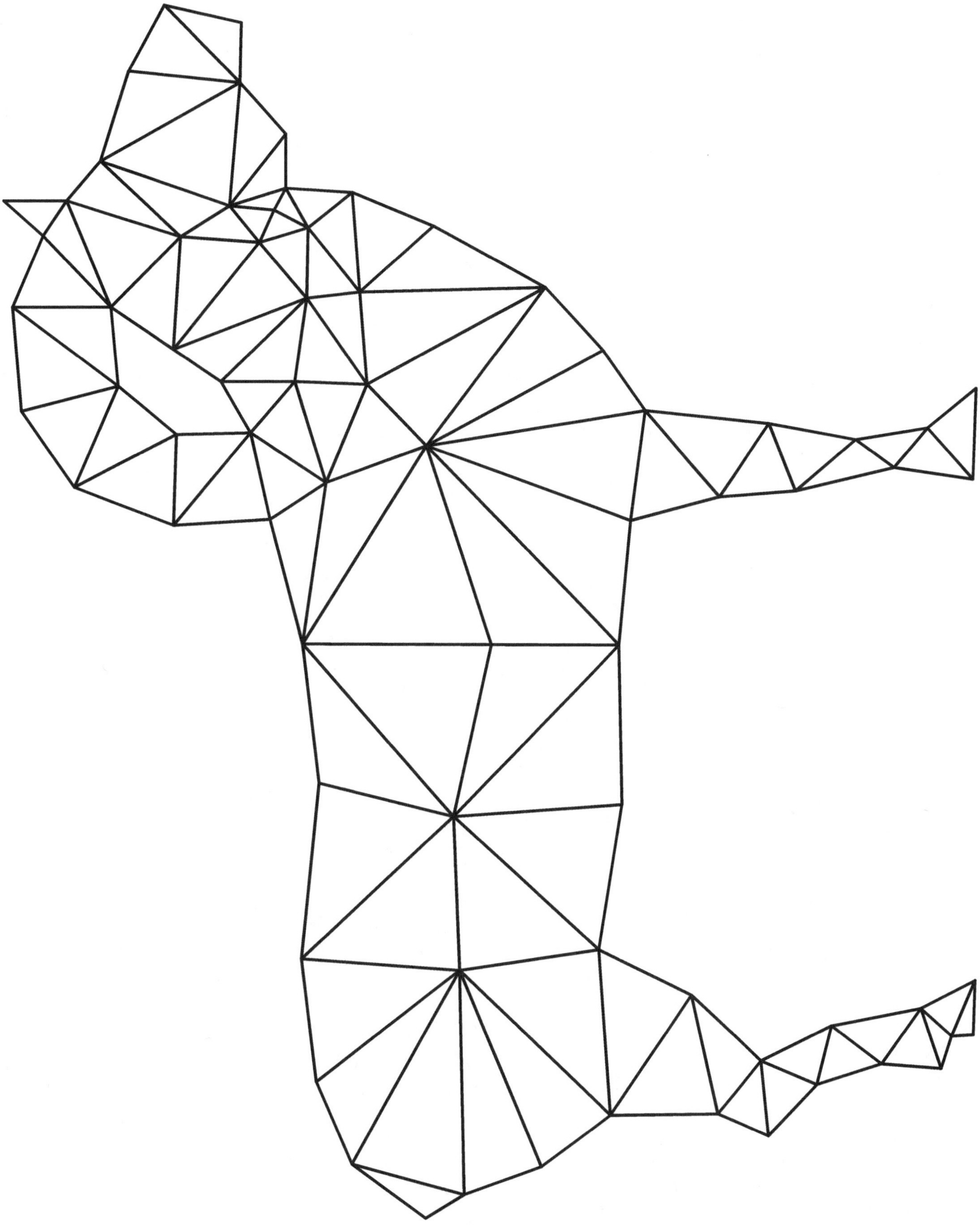

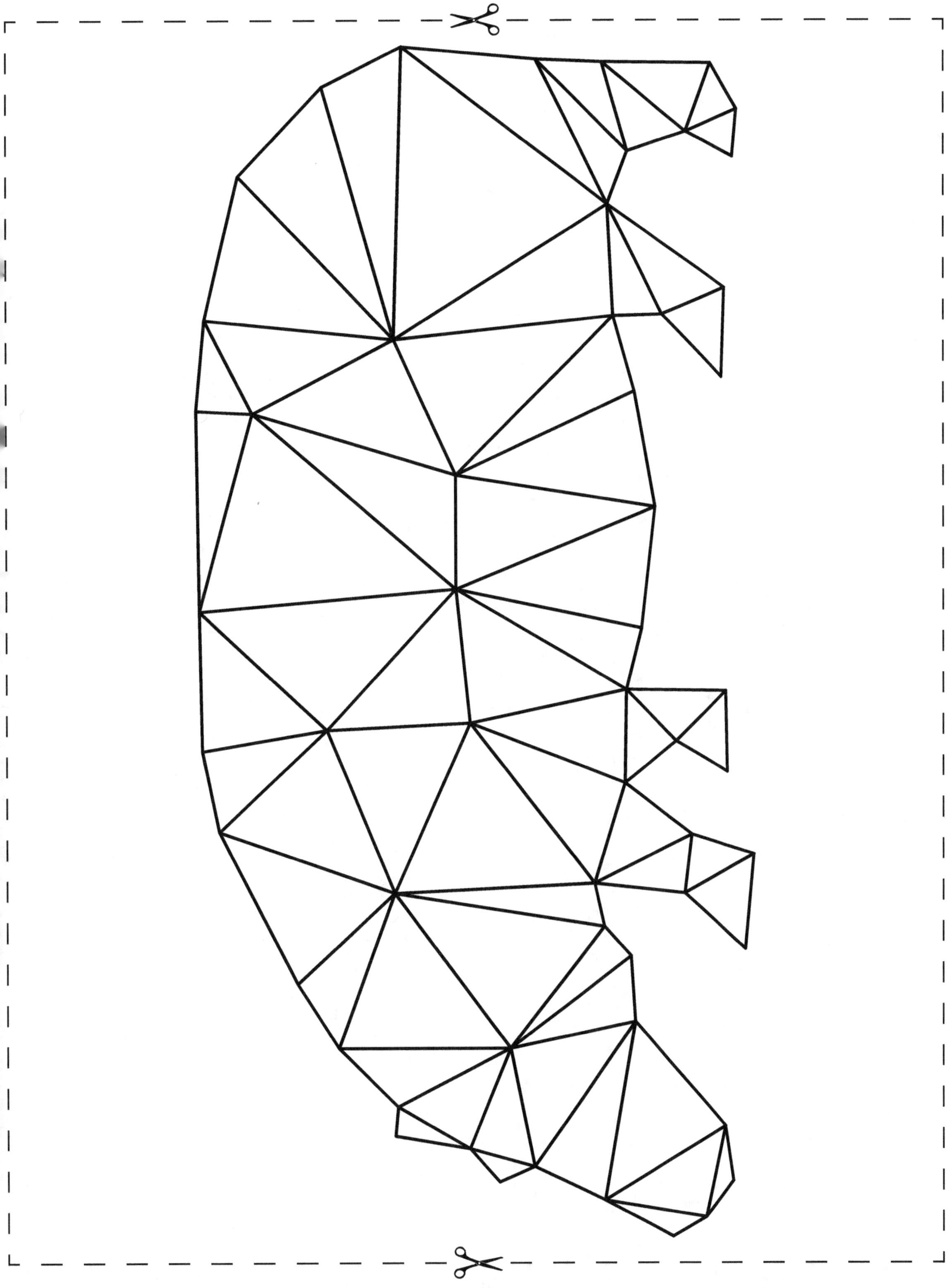

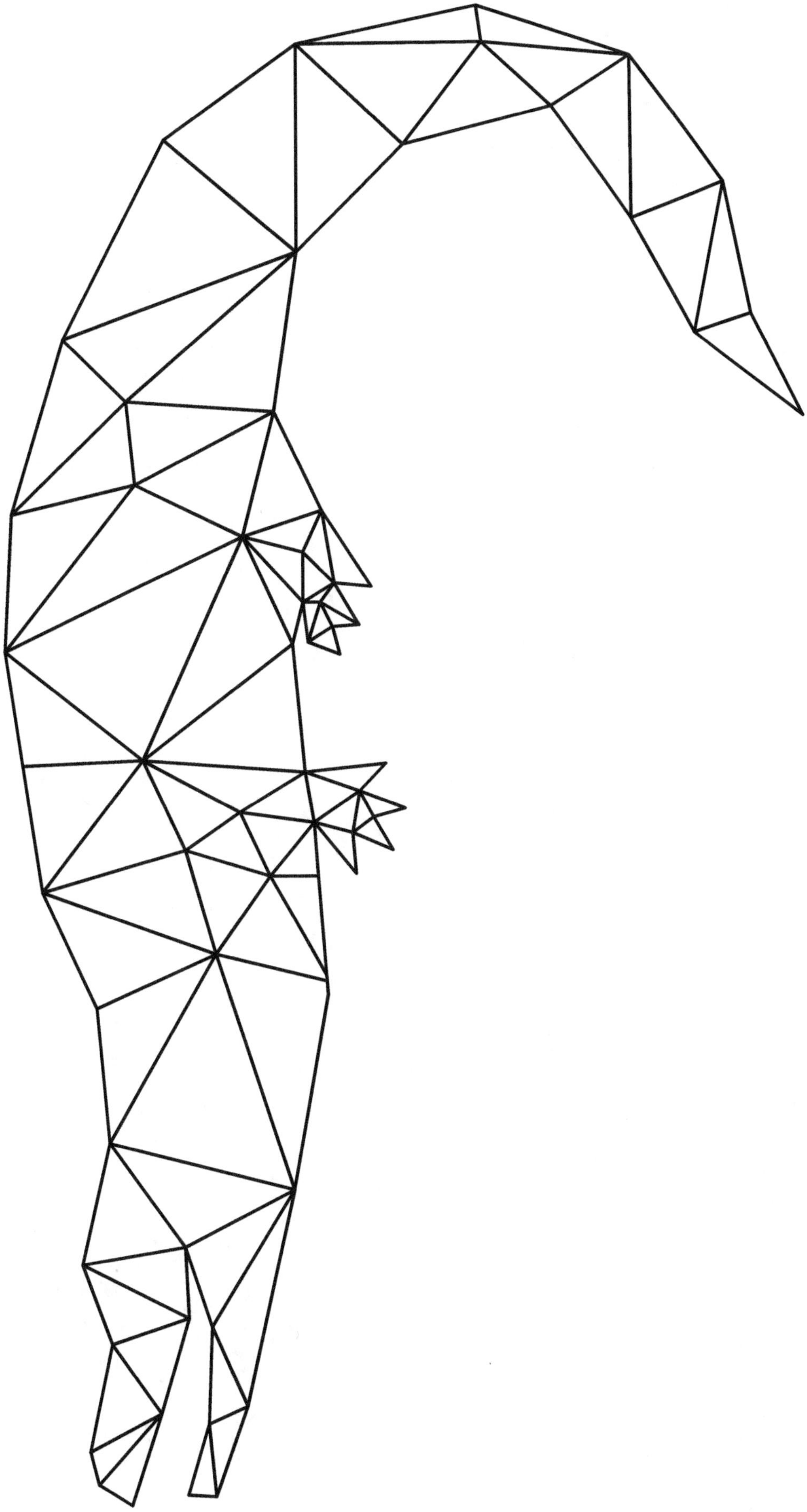

www.ingramcontent.com/pod-product-compliance
Lightning Source LLC
Chambersburg PA
CBHW060007230526
45472CB00008B/1979
* 9 7 9 8 4 6 2 5 1 2 2 6 1 *